PRESIDENTIAL
★ PETS ★

GROSSET & DUNLAP
Published by the Penguin Group
Penguin Group (USA) Inc., 375 Hudson Street, New York,
New York 10014, USA
Penguin Group (Canada), 90 Eglinton Avenue East, Suite 700,
Toronto, Ontario M4P 2Y3, Canada
(a division of Pearson Penguin Canada Inc.)
Penguin Books Ltd., 80 Strand, London WC2R 0RL, England
Penguin Group Ireland, 25 St. Stephen's Green, Dublin 2, Ireland
(a division of Penguin Books Ltd.)
Penguin Group (Australia), 250 Camberwell Road,
Camberwell, Victoria 3124, Australia
(a division of Pearson Australia Group Pty. Ltd.)
Penguin Books India Pvt. Ltd., 11 Community Centre, Panchsheel Park,
New Delhi—110 017, India
Penguin Group (NZ), 67 Apollo Drive, Rosedale,
North Shore 0632, New Zealand
(a division of Pearson New Zealand Ltd.)
Penguin Books (South Africa) (Pty.) Ltd., 24 Sturdee Avenue,
Rosebank, Johannesburg 2196, South Africa

Penguin Books Ltd., Registered Offices:
80 Strand, London WC2R 0RL, England

Photo credits: cover: Mandel Ngan/AFP/Getty Images; page 5: AP Photo/Pablo
Martinez Monsivais; page 12: AP Photo/J. Scott Applewhite, File; page 14:
Photo by David Valdez/White House/Time Life Pictures/Getty Images; page 15:
AP Photo/White House, David Valdez; page 19: Photo by Diana Walker/Time
Life Pictures/Getty Images; page 24: Courtesy of the Library of Congress; pages
26-27: Courtesy of the Library of Congress; page 28: Courtesy of the Library
of Congress; page 36: AP Photo; page 47: Courtesy of the Library of Congress;
page 52: Photo by George Skadding/Time & Life Pictures/Getty Images; page
59: Courtesy of the Library of Congress; page 62: AP Photo/Ron Edmonds;
page 63: Photo by Pete Souza/The White House via Getty Images; page 64:
Photo by Alex Wong/Getty Images

Library of Congress Control Number: 2009011514

ISBN 978-0-448-45250-0   10 9 8 7 6 5 4 3 2 1

PRESIDENTIAL
★ PETS ★

By Laura Driscoll
Illustrated by Christian Slade
and with photographs

Grosset & Dunlap

★ New Life, New Pet! ★

November 4, 2008, was a night of big changes. Barack Obama had just been elected the first African-American president of the United States. He and his wife, Michelle Obama, and their young daughters, Malia and Sasha, were going to be the country's next First Family. They would soon leave their home in Chicago and move into the White House in Washington, D.C. Sasha and Malia would start a new school. As the First Lady, their mom would become one of the busiest and most famous women in the world. Their dad was going to have the most important job in America.

In his victory speech, Barack Obama said, "Sasha and Malia, I love you both so much, and you have earned the new puppy that's coming with us to the White House."

This was big news for Sasha and Malia. But over the years, First Families have had all kinds of pets: dogs, cats, mice, snakes, birds, elephants, sheep, horses, a hyena, a hippo, and even an alligator! Only *three* presidents in US history did not have a pet in the White House.

Andrew Johnson

John Quincy Adams

Theodore Roosevelt

John F. Kennedy

George W. Bush

George Washington

So why have pets been so popular with First Families? Maybe it is because pets can make a big house—like the White House—feel more like a cozy home. Pets can force a busy president to make time for fun. And pets can give friendship to someone doing a hard and sometimes lonely job.

★ A President's Best Friend ★

President Calvin Coolidge and Rob Roy

Can you guess the most popular White House pet over the years? The dog, of course. In fact, every president for the last ninety years has had a dog. From terriers to retrievers, spaniels to collies, each pet has had a personality as unique as his or her president.

During his time in the White House, George W. Bush (president from 2001-2009) had three dogs. One was a Scottish terrier named Barney.

Barney's biggest claim to fame was as the star of "Barney Cam." For Christmas in 2002, Barney shuffled around the White House with a tiny camera attached to his collar. He filmed a "dog's eye view" of the holiday decorations. This footage was added to the Bush family's Christmas video and was put on the Internet. Millions of people watched and loved it!

After that, Barney Cam became a Christmas tradition in the Bush White House. Famous singers and athletes even appeared in some of Barney's videos.

In 2005, the Bushes got another Scottish terrier named Miss Beazley. She came to the White House as a ten-week-old puppy. Next to Barney, "Beezie" looked tiny. But a few loud barks at Barney told him she was no pushover.

President George W. Bush and Barney

Before either Barney or Miss Beazley
arrived, there was Spot, an English
springer spaniel. "Spotty" and Barney were
good pals. The president sometimes took
them on trips together in Marine One, the
presidential helicopter. Spot usually got on
without a fuss. But Barney? The president
sometimes had to chase him around the
lawn before he would go aboard.

Spot's mother, Millie, belonged to another First Family. Millie lived in the White House when George W. Bush's father was president. His name was almost the same: George H. W. Bush (1989-1993).

President George H. W. Bush and Millie in the Oval Office

First Lady Barbara Bush, one of her granddaughters, and Millie and her puppies

While Millie lived at the White House, she gave birth to Spot and her five brothers and sisters.

Besides being a mom, Millie was a best-selling author! *Millie's Book: As Dictated to Barbara Bush* was published in 1990. It sold more copies than a book the president wrote!

President Bill Clinton (1993-2001), First Lady Hillary Clinton, and their twelve-year-old daughter, Chelsea, came to the White House with only one pet— a cat named Socks.

Socks had joined the Clinton family about two years earlier. Chelsea was at her piano teacher's house for a lesson. Socks, then a stray kitten, was playing in the teacher's yard. When Chelsea held her hands out to the kitten, he jumped right into her arms! Even though Chelsea's parents were allergic to cats, they couldn't resist adding the kitten to their family.

As the First Pet, Socks became famous overnight. Letters to Socks poured in from his fans—especially kids. Some asked Socks to send them his "pawtograph."

Five years after moving into the White House, the Clinton family became dog owners. Buddy, a chocolate Labrador retriever, was just a puppy when he arrived at the White House.

Right from the start, he and the president were good friends. Buddy spent much of his time napping behind the president's desk in the Oval Office. At least once a day, Buddy dropped his ball at President Clinton's feet and started barking. He wouldn't stop until Clinton came outside to play fetch.

Unfortunately, Buddy and Socks did
not get along very well. The first time
they met, Socks hissed at Buddy and
Buddy barked at Socks.

One day, Socks swatted Buddy on
the nose. Buddy yelped and ran away.
Strangely, Buddy seemed to warm up to
Socks after that. Socks, however, never
wanted much to do with Buddy.

Later, Mrs. Clinton said that she got the feeling that a Labrador retriever was not the little brother Socks had always wanted. What would Socks have thought if the president had brought home a goat, an alligator, or elephants? Good thing he didn't live with any of the presidents in the next chapter.

★ Wild Pets of the Past ★

The White House hadn't been built when George Washington (1789-1797) became the first president, but he did have a stable full of horses and a kennel full of hounds—nearly twelve horses and forty dogs. Washington used the horses and hounds to hunt foxes, so there's nothing *too* wild about the very first presidential pets . . . except some of the dogs' names: Sweetlips, Truelove, and Madam Moose.

President Warren Harding (1921-1923) was very fond of a squirrel named Pete. Pete lived on the White House grounds. When people came to the White House for a meeting, they often brought Pete a few nuts.

Pete the squirrel and a visitor to the White House

Some unusual White House pets had special jobs. President William Taft (1909-1913) liked fresh milk. So he kept his own cow, Pauline Wayne, on the White House lawn. Each day, Pauline's milk was on the president's table.

When President Woodrow Wilson (1913-1921) looked out the windows of the White House, he'd see his flock of sheep grazing on the lawn. At the time, the United States was at war, so people

were living simply and saving money. The sheep nibbled on the grass, so the lawn didn't have to be cut. They provided mountains of wool, too!

President Benjamin Harrison (1889-1893) had a pet goat named Old Whiskers. The goat was often hitched to a cart and pulled the Harrison grandchildren around the White House grounds.

One day, the goat was pulling the president's young grandson around the lawn. All of a sudden, the goat dashed through an open gate and took off down the street. President Harrison saw what happened and chased after the goat, waving his cane and shouting all the way. Luckily, the president ran fast enough to catch up to the runaway animal.

Most people try to get rid of mice in their houses. Not President Andrew Johnson (1865-1869). One summer, he discovered a family of mice living in his bedroom. The president didn't want them to go hungry. So instead of shooing them out, Johnson left out handfuls of flour and bowls of water.

Presidents are often given animals as gifts. In 1863, a friend sent President Abraham Lincoln (1861-1865) a live turkey. It was intended to be the meal at a holiday dinner. But President Lincoln's ten-year-old son, Tad, became fond of the turkey. Tad named him Jack and begged his father to let the turkey live. Lincoln agreed, and Tad got to keep Jack as a pet.

Another wild pet lived in the White House with President John Quincy Adams (1825-1829). In 1826, a French war hero named Marquis de Lafayette came to visit—and brought an alligator with him! According to one story, the alligator lived in the East Room of the White House for two whole months!

When Lafayette left, he took the alligator
with him. Luckily, President Adams and
his wife still had their pet silkworms to
keep them company. Watching them
spin silk for the First Lady's dresses was
not quite as exciting as an alligator, but
certainly a lot safer.

The King of Siam (now called Thailand) gave President James Buchanan (1857-1861) two elephants. It seems Buchanan quickly decided the White House wasn't the best home for them because he sent them to live at the zoo.

★ Full Houses ★

Some First Families were such animal lovers that they nearly had their own zoo at the White House. President John F. Kennedy had more than twenty pets. Calvin Coolidge had about twenty-five. And President Theodore Roosevelt had more than forty! During these presidencies, you may have wondered who was in charge of the White House: the people or the animals?

President John F. Kennedy (1961-1963) and First Lady Jacqueline Kennedy, each had many pets growing up. So they surrounded their own young children, Caroline and John Jr., with pets in the White House.

The Kennedy family and many of their dogs. Their first dog, Charlie, is in the bottom left corner.

The family arrived at the White House in 1961 with a dog named Charlie. But before long, the canine pack had grown to five. There was also a cat named Tom Kitten. But the president was allergic to him, so Tom had to go live with Mrs. Kennedy's secretary.

For a short time, the family kept ducks on the White House lawn. But Charlie was always trying to catch one. And when the ducks started eating the tulips, the Kennedys found another home for them, too.

Two deer replaced the ducks—until Mrs. Kennedy was warned that although deer seemed gentle, they weren't good pets for children. So off the deer went to the Tisch Children's Zoo at Central Park in New York City.

Plenty of other animals were there to stay though. There were five horses, including Caroline's pony, Macaroni. The pony got thousands of fan letters from people around the country.

Caroline also took care of the family's parakeets, Maybelle and Bluebell. There were at least two hamsters, a rabbit named Zsa Zsa who could play a few notes on a toy horn, and more!

President Theodore Roosevelt (1901-1909) had more than forty pets while living in the White House! Actually, many of them belonged to his six children. But the president loved having the animals around as much as his kids did. There was Ted's macaw, Archie's pony, guinea pigs, a badger, a one-legged rooster, a pig, a raccoon, cats, dogs, and rats. There was also a lion, a hyena, a zebra, and bears, but these were sent to live at the family's summer house in Long Island, New York.

Algonquin, a pony, was especially loved by the Roosevelt children. One day, when little Archie Roosevelt was sick in bed, his five-year-old brother, Quentin, decided to cheer him up. Quentin took Algonquin on a ride in the White House elevator to visit Archie!

A new pet unexpectedly joined the Roosevelt family in 1903. While the president was visiting Kansas by train, a little girl offered the president a baby badger. President Roosevelt couldn't resist! His kids had many pets, but not a badger! He thanked the girl and gave her a tour of the presidential train car. Later on his train trip, he wrote a letter to his children about the pet badger he was bringing home with him.

Snakes were also popular in Roosevelt's White House. Alice, a very wild child, had a snake named Emily Spinach. Some stories say that Alice often kept the snake around her neck or in her purse just to shock people.

Quentin was also fond of snakes. Once, when the president was in an important meeting, Quentin roller-skated into the Oval Office. He had three snakes twined around his arms! At first, the men thought the snakes were toys—until they got a closer look. The visitors got a huge shock, while the president got a big laugh!

With so many pets and so many children, there was hardly ever a dull moment while the Roosevelts lived in the White House.

Calvin Coolidge (1923-1929) had a large
collection of pets. Most of the wild ones
were sent as gifts: a bear from Mexico,
a small hippo from South Africa, and a
wallaby from Australia. As much as they
loved animals, the president and First
Lady sent most of their wild pets to live at
the zoo.

But one wild critter, a raccoon, won the heart of President Coolidge and found a home in the White House—for a short time. The Coolidges named the raccoon Rebecca and built her a special house in one of the big trees on the White House grounds. Outside, they kept her leashed. Inside, Rebecca could roam freely about the White House. She loved to take long baths with a bar of soap as a bath toy. First Lady Grace Coolidge fed Rebecca shrimp and persimmon. President Coolidge took Rebecca on evening walks.

Some people who worked in the White House did not like Rebecca as much as the Coolidges. That was because she dug up houseplants, unscrewed light bulbs, and tore at clothing. But the Coolidges loved Rebecca so much that they took her on their summer vacation.

Rebecca the raccoon and First Lady Grace Coolidge

President Coolidge thought dogs were a must! He said, "Any man who does not like dogs . . . does not deserve to be in the White House." Many dogs spent time in the Coolidge White House. But the president's favorite was a snowy white collie named Rob Roy. He slept in the president's bedroom and went with him to the Oval Office. Rob Roy appears with the First Lady in a painting that still hangs in the White House. Rob Roy had to sit still for a very long time as the artist painted his portrait. To keep the frisky dog from moving, Mrs. Coolidge fed him candy!

★ First Pets Go First Class ★

What makes a pet lover smile? Seeing
their animal friends happy, of course!
Most pets enjoy the basics: good food, a
warm home, and a cozy place to sleep.
But some lucky pets—like the ones who
live in the White House—get the "royal"
treatment. That includes gourmet meals,
fancy toys, vacations to amazing places,
and a special place beside the president.

President Thomas Jefferson (1801-1809) had at least four mockingbirds. But one, who he named Dick, was his very favorite. When the president was alone in his office, he would open Dick's cage and let him fly around. The bird often landed on Jefferson's shoulder or desk and sang to him.

At mealtimes, Jefferson held small bits
of food between his lips for Dick to take.
And when the president went up to his
bedroom, Dick went, too, hopping up
the stairs after him. Sometimes Dick even
sang Jefferson to sleep.

Fala, a black Scottish terrier, was a gift to President Franklin Delano Roosevelt (1933-1945). The dog slept in a special bed at the foot of the president's bed.

Each morning, the president's breakfast was brought up to him on a tray. And each morning, there was a bone for Fala on the tray, too. Fala also got a full dinner in the evening. And all day long, he enjoyed treats from the White House staff. In time, he had to be put on a diet because he was eating too much food!

Fala often traveled with the president. In 1944, he sailed with Roosevelt all the way to some islands in the Pacific Ocean. At the time, Roosevelt, a Democrat, was running for reelection. A rumor spread that Fala had been left behind by mistake on one of the islands. The Republicans accused the president of sending a Navy ship back for the dog. They said it had cost American taxpayers millions of dollars! The story was not true.

Roosevelt said that he expected attacks during the election year. But, he said, Fala was not so understanding. Roosevelt went on to win the election and Fala became even more beloved. He got more fan mail than the president. Fala even had his own secretary to help him answer it all.

President Warren Harding's (1921-1923) dog Laddie Boy was another pampered pooch. The president took the dog with him almost everywhere. Laddie Boy even had his own chair to sit in at important meetings.

Each year, the Hardings celebrated
Laddie Boy's birthday with a big party.
They invited all of the dogs from the
neighborhood. A birthday cake made of
dog biscuits—sometimes several layers
high—was served to the animal guests.

One year, Laddie Boy was even the host of the annual Easter Egg Roll on the White House lawn. "It wouldn't have been a children's party without Laddie Boy," a *New York Times* reporter wrote. "There was almost as large a crowd of youngsters watching [Laddie Boy] as there was around the five truckloads of bottled pop in the driveway."

Some say Laddie Boy was the White House's first celebrity dog! Newspapers wrote many articles about Laddie Boy— especially when he first came to live at the White House. President Harding liked having a famous dog. He sometimes wrote letters to the press, pretending to be Laddie Boy.

Laddie Boy at the 1923 White House Easter Egg Roll

President Harding had once worked in the newspaper business. When he died in 1923, young newsboys (or paper sellers) around the country each sent in a penny. All 19,000 pennies were melted down and made into a statue of the president's beloved Laddie Boy.

Laddie Boy

★ Wanted: One Presidential Pooch ★

Barack Obama was elected president in November 2008. Even though he wouldn't become president until January 2009, he needed to get right to work! Obama immediately began to choose who would work with him in the White House. But choosing a puppy for his family took him even longer. In January, the Obamas moved into the White House—but without a dog. People asked President Obama about the puppy nearly everywhere he went: at press conferences, during TV interviews, and even on a trip to Europe.

It wasn't until April that the world met the new First Dog! He was a six-month-old Portuguese water dog named Bo. His fur was all black, except for patches of white on his chest, front paws, and chin. Bo looked like he was wearing a tuxedo! He would certainly fit right in at fancy White House parties.

Malia Obama with Bo on the White House lawn

President Obama running with Bo in the White House

Bo was a gift from Senator Ted Kennedy (a brother of President John F. Kennedy) and his wife. They had three Portuguese water dogs of their own. The Kennedys told the Obamas that Portuguese water dogs were perfect for the White House because they are obedient and smart. However, they need lots of exercise. Luckily for Bo, President Obama loves to stay in shape.

Soon after Bo came to live at the White House, the Obamas took him out to meet the press. Cameras snapped. Video cameras rolled. Reporters shouted questions like, "Where will he sleep?" and "Have there been any accidents?" All eyes were on one excited little puppy as he got to know his owners and new home. It was not the first time that a First Pet had completely stolen the show. And it certainly will not be the last!